THE WAY
OF THE SANT

Praise

"This book's reader quickly becomes a listener, and the author turns into a friend and companion who speaks gently, arrestingly, and with wisdom both practical and scriptural. We are given the essence of Tulsidas's immortal work and, simultaneously, the realities of our 21st-century world. Professor Rambachan has performed quite a feat."

— Rajmohan Gandhi

Distinguished historian, biographer, research professor, former member of the Upper House of the Indian Parliament, and grandson of Mahatma Gandhi

"Dr. Anantanand Rambachan is a wise and learned scholar and teacher, who has helped to advance the fields of Hinduism, Comparative Theology, and Interreligious Studies over his long and distinguished career. In this new monograph, he gently invites us to reflect on our core convictions in dialogue with teachings that are dear to him. This book is an act of generosity and vulnerability, reflective of the core commitments of this wonderful intellectual and spiritual guide."

—Rabbi Or Rose

Founding Director, The Miller Center for Interreligious Learning & Leadership, Hebrew College

"*The Way of the Sant* is a path that beckons, inviting the reader with its inclusivity and respect for all beings. The reader comes away with the understanding that attending to virtue leads to personal inner freedom and spaciousness, uncluttered by hatred or by exterior praise or blame or by attempts to control another's conduct."

— MARIA MUTCH
Author and literary consultant

"For centuries, Sants have offered South Asians a model for what it looks like to live a good life. Now, with the help of this book, the Sant's ideals and examples are more easily available to anyone and everyone."

— SIMRAN JEET SINGH
Author and Professor of Interreligious
Histories at Union Seminary, New York

"In this insightful and elegantly written volume, Prof. Anantanand Rambachan offers a compelling exposition of the timeless wisdom of the Sant, drawing especially from Sant Tulsidas's portrayal in the Ramayana. By tracing virtues such as compassion, humility, generosity, and love through Hindu, Sikh, Buddhist, Islamic, Christian, and Jewish narratives, he demonstrates their universality with scholarly clarity. *The Way of the Sant* is a valuable contribution to comparative theology and to the study of virtue across traditions."

— IMAM DR. A. RASHIED OMAR

Associate Teaching Professor
of Islamic Studies and Peacebuilding,
University of Notre Dame

"In our severely wounded and dysfunctional twenty-first century society, we are in dire need of finding our way back to sanity and wholeness and move us in the direction of reconciliation and healing as a global family. This book lays out the virtues of the Sant, an embodiment of truth and goodness as found in the Hindu tradition, which people of all religions or of no religion may look to as a source of inspiration and empowerment, to take on the urgent tasks before us to save ourselves from collective destruction."

— RUBEN HABITO

Founding Teacher, Maria Kannon Zen Center,
and Professor Emeritus of World Religions and
Spirituality, Perkins School of Theology,
Southern Methodist University

THE WAY
OF THE SANT

VIRTUES FOR ALL HUMANITY

Anantanand
Rambachan

Albion
Andalus
Boulder, Colorado
2025

*"The old shall be renewed,
and the new shall be made holy."*

— Rabbi Avraham Yitzhak Kook

Albion-Andalus Books
P. O. Box 19852
Boulder, CO, 80308
albion-andalus.com

Design & composition by Albion-Andalus Books

Cover design by Albion-Albion Books

Front cover photo ("Goa Sunset," Nov. 2023) taken by Geeta Rambachan

ISBN: 978-1-953220-50-9

Manufactured in the U.S.A.

Bandau sant samanachitta
hita anahita nahi kou

Anjaligata subha sumana
jimi sama sugandha kara dou

I bow before the Sants
who are loving towards all
and free from enmity—
just as a beautiful flower
placed in one's palms
gives its fragrance to both.

Tulsidas

Acknowledgements

I am grateful, beyond words, to my wife Geeta who has walked every step with me in bringing this book to publication. This book is the fruit of her unwavering support, encouragement, and diligent reading. Maria Mutch, literary consultant and writer, was generous with her time and wisdom, affirmed the value of this book, and offered valuable advice for improving the manuscript. I also thank Dr. Shashikant Sane for his encouragement for the lectures on the Sant and for his faith in me. Lastly, I am grateful to Netanel Miles-Yépez and Daniel Jami for their assistance in getting this book published.

Contents

Introduction

My focus in this small book is on virtue. My intention, however, is not to discuss virtue as an abstract concept, but to consider how we may cultivate virtue in our lives, how we may embody virtue.

I am aware that the word "virtue" is not used much in popular discourse, and may even appear anachronistic and ancient. The term "values" is more familiar and widely employed. These words are often used interchangeably, but there are differences. Values may be moral, but are not necessarily so. One may describe oneself as having a value for wealth, power, or fame without any reference to morality. Virtues, on the other hand, are always morally oriented.

A virtue is a quality of character that expresses goodness in our interpersonal and social relationships. Virtues are about who we are at the deepest level of being. Virtues are intrinsically relational and promote personal and social well-being. Virtues include such qualities like compassion, humility, generosity, and honesty.

Virtues do not usually change over time, even though the ways in which we express these in our lives may change. If we think of life as a tree, virtues are the roots that ground the tree firmly, allowing it to grow and flourish. Values, on the other hand, may be more subject to change and cultural influence. While values may be inherited culturally, virtues must be cultivated through mindful practice.

I hope, dear reader, that you are not deterred by my use of the word "virtue." I hope you see this book as a warm and gentle invitation, to both heart and mind, in conversation with the Sant, to consider the core moral commitments that you express in your relationships as you journey through life. My aim here is not to prescribe normative virtues for you to judge yourself, but to open a window to the beauty and fragrance of virtue manifested in the way of the Sant. The appeal of virtue is beauty and not fear. Virtues cannot be coerced. Virtues are meaningful only when embraced in freedom.

The way of the Sant is a lifelong journey of learning and growth. It is one on which we must learn to be gentle and forgiving with ourselves, even as we forgive others. The aim is the cultivation of virtue through self-understanding and not self-condemnation. It is the way of self-acceptance with all our human frailties and not one of self-deprecation or rejection. It is awakening to a life of beauty through the love and practice of virtue.

In the Hindu tradition, and also in other traditions, religious knowledge is not personally meaningful unless it expresses itself in a way of being. In the matter of virtue, we must become what we know to be good. In the *Mundaka Upanishad*, we have a beautiful statement, *brahma veda brahmaiva bhavati.* The teaching here is that when we know the Divine, we are transformed into Divinity. We express Divinity in our way of being in the world.

Where do we turn to learn about what it means to be a virtuous human being? Who are our teachers and mentors? Most of us are not and will not be renunciants. Our context is a different one. We are mothers and fathers, sons and daughters, husbands and wives. We are active in our professions and in our communities. We are involved in relationships of various kinds, and it is in these relationships that we must practice virtue. Where may we find models of virtue who are immersed in life?

Traditionally, Hindu monks severed their ties with family and community, moved away from their birth places, and became homeless wanderers. They relied on villagers for their daily needs, since they had relinquished the economic means to produce or purchase what they required to sustain life. We can certainly learn from monks and renunciants, but the lifestyle of the renunciant is only one way of being religious and is not an option for most of us.

Even so, what it means to be a renunciant has been changing. For instance, Swami Vivekananda, the founder of the Ramakrishna Order of renunciants, had an understanding of the role of the monk very different than that of earlier times. He wanted monks who were active in the world, committed to lives of service and engaged in delivering health care, education, and overcoming poverty.

Where do we find exemplars of virtue who are similarly immersed, like most people, in the complexities of daily life? In this book, I suggest that we turn to those in the Hindu tradition named as Sants. The figure of the Sant is widely known in the religious traditions of India. For example, in Sikhism the Sant is deeply honored. The word "Sant" is used many times in the Sikh sacred text known as the *Guru Granth Sahib*. It is used as a name for the Divine, for the ten Gurus who established the spiritual tradition, and for luminous exemplars of virtue. Sants in Sikhism are highly revered people of wisdom, humility, love, and compassion for all beings. A Sant may be a renunciant, but renunciation in the sense of monasticism and severing ties with family and community is not a required quality.

The word Sant is derived from the Sanskrit "*sat*," meaning truth or goodness. It is a title conferred by the community upon those who are experienced as embodying virtue. The closest English word is "saint," but the root meaning is different. Saint is derived from the Latin word "sanctus," suggesting holiness and sanctity, and the Catholic Church has a formal process of canonization and elevation to the status of sainthood. In the Hindu tradition, the process is informal and community based. Many Hindu writers translate "Sant" as "saint." In this work, I leave the name untranslated, even though I am certain that there are significant shared virtues among Sants and saints. The names of the Sants in the Hindu tradition are too numerous to list. They belong to all the regions of India, represent the theological diversity of Hinduism, and are both male and female.

The virtues of the Sant are described in various sacred texts, but, for this book, I draw in a special way from the description of the Sant by Sant Tulsidas (ca. 16th CE) in his version of the Ramayana that he titled the *Ramacharitamanas* (The Lake Filled with the Deeds of Rama). First written by the Sanskrit poet, Valmiki, and then in various Indian regional languages, the Ramayana tells the life story of Rama, considered by millions of Hindus, and by Tulsidas himself, as the embodiment of the Divine in our world. The version authored by Tulsidas continues to enjoy great popularity in India and in the Hindu diaspora.

To understand these virtues more fully, let us turn to the story of Rama, whose life became the canvas on which these values were so vividly painted by Tulsidas. Rama is the son of King Dasaratha of Ayodhya. As a consequence of palace intrigue and rivalries, he is banished to live an ascetic life in the forests for fourteen years. He is accompanied by his wife, Sita, and his brother, Lakshmana. During their journey into the wilderness, Sita is abducted by Ravana, king of Lanka, and kept prisoner on his island kingdom. A long search to find Sita ensues, led by Hanuman, the servant of Rama and the exemplar of love and service for God. With Hanuman's indefatigable service, Sita is located, rescued, and returns to Ayodhya with Rama.

Stories such as this are not of a distant past; they continue to shape the moral imagination of communities around the world, including my own. As Tulsidas tells Rama's story, he mines each incident and dialogue in the text for what it reveals to us about the nature of the Divine as loving and compassionate. In addition, he repeatedly turns, whenever an opportunity presents itself, to discussing the Sant as the embodiment of virtue and love for God. It is clearly one of his favorite subjects, judging by the number of times the word Sant occurs in his text. There is no end to his praise for the lives of the Sants and their value to the world. This makes his text a particularly rich resource for our study of their virtues.

In each chapter of this work, I highlight and discuss one of the prominent virtues that he associates with the Sant. Most of these virtues are taken from his discussion of the Sant in the final chapter (*Uttarakanda*) of his work. Each virtue is an invitation for your own reflection. My thoughts are only meant to be a catalyst for your own thinking.

My hope is that we see the Sants as representing a relevant and attainable way of being, and that we seek to deeply understand, contemplate, and emulate this way. This book is meant for readers who wish to understand and cultivate virtues. I believe that our world would be better by having more Sants.

This work also represents a continuation of my commentaries and public teachings on the Tulsidas text that I started in 1987, which have been published in a series of small volumes. These include, among others, *Love and Truth in the Ramayana of Tulsidas, Hanuman: the Messenger of God, Hanuman: The Devotee of God, Rama Gita, Rama Darshan, Bharata: Love and Justice in the Ramayana* and *Ravana: Power Without Virtue.* Some of my public talks on the *Ramayana* are also available in *Wisdom Teachings from the Hindu Ramayana.*

These commentaries express my love for the Tulsidas text, but also my gratitude for the role of the text in sustaining the spiritual lives of my Hindu ancestors. I was born into a Hindu family on the Caribbean island of Trinidad. My great-grandparents migrated from India during the latter part of the nineteenth century to work on British sugar plantations and to fill a labor vacuum created after the abolition of African slavery.

Most of the Indian immigrants to the Caribbean came from the North Indian regions of Uttar Pradesh and Bihar. The religious text with which they were most familiar, and which they continued to memorize, recite, and sing, was the Ramayana. It was one of the first sacred texts to which I was exposed, and the characters and events made a deep impression on my young mind. My commentaries express my gratitude to my ancestors for the preservation of the tradition of Ramayana recital and commentary. I see my work as a contribution to enriching and inviting further reflection on this tradition.

This book has its origin in a series of virtual public lectures on the Sant delivered during the years 2024-2025 under the auspices of the Hindu Society of Minnesota. I am grateful to all who attended my lectures and for the thoughtful discussions that always followed each talk. In writing this book, I attempt to preserve the conversational style of my original talks.

In this book, I draw especially on the Hindu tradition and the lives of the Sants. Yet the virtues of compassion, humility, generosity, and love are not confined to one tradition. They are the common inheritance of humanity, celebrated in the stories and teachings of many faiths. For this reason, I have also included narratives from the Sikh and Buddhist traditions, and I have extended this circle to embrace stories from Islam, Christianity, and Judaism.

My hope is that readers from different religious backgrounds will recognize in these stories the same fragrance of virtue that Tulsidas describes in the Sant. Virtue knows no boundaries of creed, culture, or nation. The way of the Sant is, in truth, a way for all humanity.

1

The Way of the Sandal Tree

Santa asantahi kai asi karani/
jimi kuthara chandana acharani
Katai parasu malaya sunu bhai/
nij guna dehi sugandha basai

The difference between a virtuous person
and one lacking in virtue
is like that of the sandal tree and the axe.
The axe cuts the sandal tree,
but the tree gives its fragrance to the axe.

Tulsidas, *Uttarakanda*

The fragrance of sandalwood is unique and
regarded as sacred. As a paste, it is applied to the
forehead during Hindu rituals to remind us of

the Divinity that abides in every heart and body. As incense, sandalwood is waved before icons *(murtis)* as an act of honor and reverence. The scent of sandalwood calms and soothes. Sandalwood fragrance endures, even as it ages, and it gives of itself to objects around it. If a chip of sandalwood is placed in a box of clothing, it imparts fragrance to everything. This is the very nature of sandalwood.

Like the fragrance of the sandalwood that shines among other fragrances, the Sant stands out among other human beings. There is a radiance, a luminosity about the Sant that, like sandalwood fragrance, touches and lights up the lives of those who come into contact with him. His goodness is as natural as the fragrance of the sandal tree. It is as impossible for a Sant not to be virtuous as it is for the sandalwood to cease giving its fragrance. He manifests goodness without expecting anything in return just as the sandal tree gives its fragrance even to the axe that cuts it.

Some may argue that it is easier to be virtuous among people who are virtuous and to be loving and kind towards those who are loving and kind towards us. How do we deal with those who lack virtue and who are inconsiderate in relationships? Could we be kind to those who are unkind? Could we love those who hate us? Could we speak gently to those who speak in anger? Could we deal justly with those who are unjust? Could we practice self-control when others around us are losing theirs? Could our words be true, pleasant, and beneficial when others speak words that are untrue, harsh, and destructive?

With the example of the sandal tree and the axe, the Sant teaches that our commitment to virtue is tested when we encounter those who care nothing for virtue. This is the central insight of the example before us. The sandal tree never wavers from its nature. It gives generously of its fragrance even to the axe that chops it. The axe comes away with its beautiful fragrance. The cruelty of the axe does not alter the sandal tree's nature of exuding sweetness. In a similar way, a Sant does not become unjust because others are unjust, does not hate because others hate, and does not speak words in anger because others do so. The goodness of the Sant is not altered by the absence of goodness in others. If the behavior of another succeeds in provoking a response in us contrary to our own wisdom and virtue, then we cede power and control to another. We are no longer faithful to ourselves.

The sandal tree always emits its fragrance, but this fragrance grows even stronger if the wood is cut or crushed. The tiniest bit of wood emits its distinctive odor. Similarly, the trials and challenges which a Sant may experience only serve to deepen and make manifest the Sant's innate goodness. The Sant does not control another's conduct, but unfailingly responds from a heart of loving goodness.

We may see this spirit in a story from the Islamic tradition about the Prophet Muhammad:

> Each morning, as he passed a certain house, a woman would empty her garbage on him. She did this not once, but day after day, with the intention of humiliating him. Muhammad, however, did not retaliate. He neither shouted at her nor returned her insult. His calmness and patience revealed a goodness that no act of malice could diminish. One morning, the garbage did not fall. Concerned, Muhammad inquired after the woman and learned that she had fallen ill. Instead of feeling relief at her absence, he went to visit her, carrying compassion in his heart. The woman, astonished, wept at his kindness.

She had sought to injure his dignity, but his response was care and gentleness. Like the sandal tree that gives fragrance to the axe that cuts it,

Muhammad gave the fragrance of love even to one who wronged him.

It is important to clarify that the goodness of the Sant is not a response of weakness or surrender in the face of violence or injustice. Injustice and untruth must always be resisted, but only with truth, love, and justice. One resists from a deep place of faithfulness to one's deepest commitments. The goodness of the Sant is a powerful manifestation of strength.

This spirit of the sandal tree is not only found in sacred texts, but also in the lives of Hindu Sants, such as Mirabai, whose response to hatred revealed only the fragrance of love. Mirabai, the 16th-century princess of Mewar, gave her heart completely to Krishna. She sang in the streets, welcomed all who came to join her in devotion, and cared little for the conventions of royal life. Her in-laws considered her behavior a disgrace and tried on several occasions to silence her, even plotting to take her life.

Tradition tells us that she was once sent a basket with a cobra hidden inside, but when she opened it, she found only a garland of flowers. On another occasion she was offered a cup of poison, yet when she drank it while singing Krishna's name, it became nectar.

Whether we understand these moments literally or as symbolic of her strength, the truth they affirm is clear: Mirabai never returned cruelty with cruelty. What others meant for harm became, for her, an occasion to turn again to Krishna. Instead of anger, she offered song; instead of bitterness, she gave love. In her life, Mirabai exemplified the way of the sandal tree: even when struck by the axe of hatred, she released only the fragrance of devotion.

Centuries later, this same fragrance of love was carried into the struggles for justice by Mahatma Gandhi and Martin Luther King Jr., who also showed the world what it means to walk the way of the sandal tree. They taught us the path of loving resistance and the strength of love.

It is important to say here that Gandhi's legacy is viewed with greater complexity today than in the past. While his teachings on nonviolence, justice, and spiritual strength remain influential, many also critique some of his views, especially around caste and race. Acknowledging this complexity allows us to receive his contributions without erasing the conversations his legacy invites.

Gandhi, who was Indian and Hindu, drew deeply from the traditions of India and the example of Jesus and his teachings in the Sermon on the Mount. Martin Luther King Jr., who was American and Christian, felt that he understood Jesus much better because of Gandhi. Let me highlight four of their shared commitments that speak of their fidelity to virtue and shed light on what the way of the sandal tree means when expressed in life.

First, for both Gandhi and Dr. King, there was nothing passive about non-violence. It is not indifference in the face of evil. Nonviolence does not ask us to suffer in silence. "No person", said Gandhi, "could be actively nonviolent and not rise against social injustice no matter where it occurred." Nonviolence, Dr. King said, "is not passive non-resistance to evil; it is active nonviolent resistance to evil." It is not for the coward; it is for the strong. Gandhi spoke of it as *satyagraha* or 'truth-force.'

Second, for Gandhi and Dr. King, nonviolence, the English word, and *ahimsa,* the Sanskrit word, are 'negative' in that they describe the absence of violence. The content, however, is positive and powerful. "In its positive form," said Gandhi, "*ahimsa* means the largest love, the greatest charity." "At the center of nonviolence," said Dr. King, "stands the principle of love." They both understood nonviolence as love in action. Nonviolence does not exclude resistance to injustice; on the contrary, it demands such resistance. What it does exclude is hate. Confronted with hate, one does not hate.

Third, for Gandhi and Dr. King, the object of loving resistance is not the human being, but the forces and systems of injustice and oppression. As

Dr. King put it, "It is the evil that the nonviolent resister seeks to defeat, not the persons victimized by evil." Gandhi distinguished between human beings and their deeds. He believed that no human being should be defined entirely by what he or she does. This distinction enabled Gandhi and King to fight and resist evil without hate and the urge to humiliate and demean those they struggled against. Each one identified the particular evil he fought against. For Dr. King it was racism, and for Gandhi it was colonial exploitation.

Fourth, for Gandhi and King, the goal of nonviolence is not domination, but the creation of communities of goodness. "The end," said Dr. King, "is redemption and reconciliation." King spoke of this community as the "beloved community;" Gandhi named it *"Ramrajya"*—the kingdom of God. It was an inclusive community of reconciliation, love, and justice. Gandhi's community included people from all of India's diverse religious traditions—Hindus, Muslims, Buddhists, Christians, and Jews. Gandhi visualized a true community as one in which people of different faiths may come to have the same regard for other faiths as they have for their own. In his ideal community, we will all be defenders and protectors of each other's rights, ready to speak out and protest when others are defamed, misrepresented, or betrayed.

The way of love, the way of the sandal tree, is a long-term vision for a flourishing community grounded in loving relationships. The way of the axe, that is the way of violence, may produce quick results, but every act of violence also encourages its future use, and does not enable the human transformation necessary for building loving communities that support the good life for all.

The way of the sandal tree is a way of life. Mahatma Gandhi and Dr. Martin Luther King Jr., by following the way of the sandal tree, advanced the creation of a better community by seeking to transform both unjust social structures and human hearts.

Consider a scene from 1963 in Birmingham, Alabama. Dr. King and civil rights marchers faced police dogs and firehoses, but did not fight back. They stood firm in nonviolence—some kneeling, others singing. The images shocked the nation. But more than that, they revealed something deeper: power without violence. King believed that this kind of moral witness had the power to change hearts, not just laws. It was the sandalwood meeting the axe.

Although the axe, from a limited and short-sighted judgment, may appear to have destroyed the sandal tree, the tree is triumphant. Its victory is found in the fact that it did not surrender its intrinsic virtue to emit and share its fragrance.

This image captures vividly what it means to honor others even in the face of harm. Similarly, the virtues by which the Sant lives, and, in many cases, dies, ultimately prevail and endure. The virtuous are the ones who live in our hearts and memories, and who are revered in history.

It is people like the Buddha, Jesus, Gandhi, and King that the thoughtful remember with love. Those who are oppressive and unjust are remembered with dishonor and contempt. It is the fragrance of our virtuous lives that live in our families and communities. The *Mundaka Upanishad* affirms this same truth in these unforgettable words: "Truth alone triumphs, never untruth (*satyam eva jayate nanrtam*)."

In a world full of axes, what kind of fragrance will we leave behind?

2

EMPATHY WITH OTHERS IN SORROW AND JOY

*Para dukha dukha/
sukha sukha dekhem para*

*Unhappy when others are unhappy
and delighting in their joy.*

Tulsidas, *Uttarakanda*

In Chapter 1, we considered Tulsidas' likening of the Sant to the sandal tree that gives its fragrant odor to the axe that cuts it. Even the cruelty of the axe cannot alter the nature of the sandal tree to emit its beautiful scent. The tree remains unwavering in its fidelity to giving its beauty to others. In a similar way, a Sant does not become unjust because others are unjust, does not hate because others hate, and does not speak angry words because others do so. The goodness of the Sant is not altered by the lack of goodness in others.

In this Chapter, I invite you to consider with me a second virtue of the Sant offered to us by Tulsidas. He describes the Sant as being unhappy when others are unhappy and as delighting in the joy of others (*para dukkha dukkha/sukha sukha dekhem para*). In another place in his text, he uses a most beautiful analogy to describe the heart of the Sant. Many poets, according to Tulsidas, have compared the Sant's heart to the softness of butter. This comparison, Tulsidas says, misses a significant difference. Butter melts when it experiences the heat of the sun. In other words, butter melts over its own suffering. The Sant's heart, on the other hand, melts when others suffer.

The importance of Tulsidas' description of the Sant as identifying with others in sorrow and happiness is better appreciated in contrast with certain popular notions of spiritual people as withdrawn from the world, severing relationships, aloof and untouched by the suffering of others. The traditional renunciant in Hinduism severed ties with family and community, gave up his profession, dissolved his marriage, distributed property to his heirs, and adopted a wandering lifestyle. His (usually male) identity was no longer connected with family and community, and this was signified by adopting a new name. His singular concern was the pursuit of personal spiritual liberation. In the Sant, however, we have a description of a spiritual person as one who is moved by the suffering of others; she or he suffers when they suffer and rejoices with them in happiness. The Sant is a caring being, whose eyes and heart are open to the world and to the experiences of others.

In Chapter 6:22 of the *Bhagavadgita*, there is an important verse describing the state of liberation (*moksha*):

> Having attained that state [of liberation], one does not regard any gain to be greater. Established in this, one remains unmoved by even the greatest sorrow.

The commentators on this verse generally focus their remarks on the description of the liberated person as unmoved even by the heaviest of sorrows. Tulsidas' portrait of the Sant as suffering and rejoicing with others adds a very important clarification of the *Bhagavadgita's* description, which may be too easily read as justifying a lack of concern for others. Although a liberated person may exemplify heroic strength in dealing with personal suffering, this does not imply that such a person remains unaffected when others suffer.

Freedom from personal unhappiness does not mean that one ceases to be moved by the sorrow of others. Tulsidas' insight on this point is most valuable and needs more emphasis.

We see Tulsidas' understanding manifested in the lives of some of the great Hindu teachers. Ramana Maharshi (1879-1950), for instance, suffered from a very painful form of cancer during the last years of his life. He had several surgeries that failed to halt the progression of his cancer. In spite of the intense pain, and without access to modern pain medications, Ramana never complained. In fact, he had to console those who were pained by his physical suffering and declining health. Ramana never ceased, however, to be moved by the suffering of others.

His biographers tell of his relationship with a young woman, Echammal, who was twenty-five years old when she lost both her husband and only son.

> In her grief, she visited Ramana seeking comfort and became his disciple. With his permission, Echammal adopted a daughter. When the time was appropriate, she arranged a marriage for her daughter, and named her grandson Ramana.

Tragically, one day, Echammal
received the news, by telegram, that
her daughter had passed away. She
raced up to Ramana Maharshi with
the telegram in hand. Ramana took
it from her and read its contents
with tears flowing from his eyes.
After the funeral of her daughter,
Echammal returned to Ramana and
placed her grandson in his arms. He
held the child gently to his bosom
and again wept.

Ramana's deep wisdom and elevated spiritual
state did not constrict and render his heart
incapable of experiencing and sharing the pain
of another. On the contrary, his spirituality and
wisdom manifested in a beautiful tenderness of
heart that, in the words of Tulsidas, melted for
others. I describe this incident in the life of one of
the greatest contemporary Hindu teachers since
it demonstrates, so powerfully, that the fruit of
wisdom is not a cold aloof heart, but a tender heart
open to the suffering of others.

Tulsidas' description of the Sant as identifying
with others in joy and sorrow is unqualified. If the
Sant is an American national, Tulsidas does not
suggest that the Sant feels sorrow only when an
American suffers or rejoices only when Americans

are happy. He does not privilege or prioritize any nationality. He does not limit the Sant's empathy for people by race, ethnicity, religion, age, or gender. *"Para"* simply means "another." The ability of the Sant to identify with others in suffering and joy is not impeded by any particular identity.

It is also true, however, that we identify more easily with the suffering and joy of those we know well, such as members of our family, our community, or our nation. While this is natural, it is problematic if the circle of our identity does not expand. Tulsidas is speaking about the disposition of the heart. We are not growing spiritually if our hearts respond only to the suffering of our own family, or to the suffering of members of our own country or religion. Something is profoundly wrong spiritually if my heart is pained by the hunger of my own child, but I am indifferent to a starving child elsewhere. To walk the path of the Sant is to have an expansive heart and not a narrow and constricted one. The Sant is moved by suffering—wherever it occurs and whoever suffers. The Sant's identity with others is universal.

This quality of shared joy and sorrow is memorably expressed in the 15th century by the poet-saint Narsinh Mehta, who was himself accorded the title of Sant. In one of his famous songs, "Who Is the Worshipper of God? (*Vaishnavajan To*)," he answered his question in a succinct line, "One who knows the pain of another." The knowing of which Narsinh Mehta speaks is not just knowing about or receiving information about another's suffering. Each day, for example, by listening to the news on television or by reading the newspaper, we learn about the pain of others. Such information may have a momentary impact on us, but the suffering of the other recedes from our minds with the changing of the channel or the turning of the page. The effects are momentary.

The knowing of which Narsinh sings and Tulsidas writes is more profound and significant. Knowing here is not just receiving information in the mind, but a movement of the heart that enables us to identify deeply with another. Knowing is loving, the ability to see oneself in the other. Knowing here inspires action. It is identical with compassion, which literally means "suffering with" (from the Latin *com*, meaning 'with' and *passio* meaning 'suffering').

We find the same truth affirmed in the *Bhagavadgita* (6:32), where Krishna describes the best Yogi as the one who has cultivated the capacity to see herself in the joy and sorrow of others. This identity expresses itself outwardly in appropriate actions to relieve suffering. In the song of Narsinh Mehta mentioned above, he adds that the worshipper who knows the pain of another strives actively on his or her behalf, free from arrogance and thoughts of self-benefit. Tulsidas echoes this teaching, reminding us that those who love God are actively devoted to the wellbeing of others, compassionate, and united with them in suffering *(ram bhagat parahit nirat para dukha dukhi dayal)*.

What Tulsidas makes clear is that spiritual growth is not growth in indifference and an uncaring attitude towards our fellow human beings. It is not withdrawal from the world. It is not about building a wall around oneself that enables one to be unaffected by the lives of others. It is unfortunate that many of us in the Hindu tradition have the impression that the closer we are to God, the further away we are from the world, from human relationships, and from concern about others. Or perhaps we believe that in order to grow closer to God, we need to turn our backs on the world and on our fellow human beings.

In describing the Sant, Tulsidas reminds us that compassion and the readiness to alleviate the suffering of others are at the heart of the religious life. Spiritual growth is the expansion of the heart in love. The ideal that this verse offers to us is a love without boundaries—a love uninhibited by geography, nation, language, culture, or ethnicity. Here, the inner and outward dimensions are complementary. The inner transformation of the heart expresses itself in outward actions of care and service.

Identifying with others in suffering may indeed seem challenging in a world so full of suffering and need. It is natural that we may even experience fear about the high demands made on us, emotionally and otherwise. How do we remain whole and centered and avoid inward disintegration? It is important, I want to suggest, that we acknowledge, in humility, our human limits. Even as our hearts are moved by suffering occurring anywhere, our ability to move from empathy to action is limited by our finite resources and capacities. This is a healthy realism and not a reason for self-deprecation. On the other hand, however, the magnitude of suffering in our world is no justification for total inaction. Our efforts in limited spaces are still invaluable.

The Sant's ability to identify with others in suffering does not spring from inner weakness. It expresses the Sant's strength and deep centeredness in the fullness of the Divine, who the Sant sees in every being. Through this seeing, the Sant feels united with everyone. The Sant's compassion expresses the steadiness of being anchored in God. Established in the Divine, the Sant is nourished by an everflowing source of love and energy that expresses itself in his or her relationships with others.

Having the Divine as her safe haven enables the Sant to be a source of support and refuge for others. Standing on the firm ground of an all-pervasive

Divinity, the Sant can extend a hand to lift others without being dragged into and swept in the turbulent river of life. Similarly, our own ability to be sources of support and sustenance to others is enhanced by grounding ourselves in the Divine. We must not be fearful that identification with others in suffering is self-destructive.

It is unfortunate that we live in times when the constricted heart is praised. We are encouraged to put the interests of our nation above the interest of all other nations, even if such narrowness causes suffering. In a similar way, we are encouraged to put the interests of our own religious and ethnic communities above all others. National and personal interests are not unimportant, but these ought not to be championed in ways that are reckless and indifferent to the suffering of others. The way of the Sant is the way of concern for the universal community of living beings.

3

WITHOUT ENEMIES

Sama Abhutaripu

Seeing Equally and Without Enemies

Tulsidas, *Uttarakanda*

In Chapter 2, we discussed the Sant as identifying with others in joy and in sorrow. We recalled Narsinh Mehta's poetry and his definition of the lover of God as a knower of the pain of others. The lover finds delight in freeing others from suffering without thoughts of reward or self-righteousness. The *Maha Upanishad* teaches that the empathy of a constricted heart is limited to particular relationships—"These are the ones I care about; I do not care about others." On the other hand, the empathy of the expansive heart is inclusive and sees the entire world as one family (*vasudhaiva kutumbakam*). This is the heart of the Sant.

In this Chapter, I invite you to consider with me a third virtue of the Sant, described by Tulsidas as being "one without enemies (*sama abhutaripu*)." We have similar expressions in other sacred texts. In Chapter 12 of the *Bhagavadgita*, Shri Krishna, the Divine teacher of Arjuna, speaks of the people dear to his heart. He describes such people as having no hate for anyone *(advesta sarva bhutanam)* and as same-minded to enemy and friend *(samah shatrau cha mitre cha)*.

To understand this virtue of the Sant, I think that a few important clarifications are needed. First, this virtue, and others described by Tulsidas, speak specifically to interpersonal relationships. Tulsidas is not speaking about relationships between states, kingdoms, or organizations. Though, I think that states and organizations have a lot to learn from the way of the Sant, and should give more thought to the practice of these virtues. In relationships between states and organizations, there should also be no place for hate or for the enemy mentality. This mentality sometimes gets transmitted across generations and adds to the difficulties and challenges of peacemaking.

Second, the statement "without enemies," is not naïve or unrealistic. It does not deny the existence of people who may see and treat the Sant as an enemy. The phrase, after all, admits the existence of such people. Others may regard the Sant as their enemy, but the Sant does not regard or treat anyone as an enemy. The Sant is free from the enemy mentality.

Third, if the Sant is free from the enemy mentality, that which we speak of as *shatru buddhi*, what exactly is this mentality? What does it mean to think of another as one's enemy (*shatru*)? A friend (*mitra*) is someone who desires your happiness and wellbeing and acts appropriately to fulfill this desire. An enemy, on the other hand, is one who desires and acts to cause you pain and delights in seeing you hurt.

Generally, our disposition towards those we perceive as enemies is one of hate (*dvesha*). *Dvesha* is a mental and emotional condition of intense dislike towards another. It is usually accompanied by anger and a desire for the defeat and humiliation of the other. Hate may be focused on individuals, but it may also be focused on internal groups or citizens of another nation. It is often, as noted already, transmitted from one generation to another. Examples include racism, xenophobia, homophobia, anti-Semitism, Islamophobia, Hinduphobia, or other forms of antagonism to entire groups. Today, there is a growing rhetoric of hate against migrants and refugees who come to our borders in desperation and need.

While recognizing that there are people who may regard her as an enemy and wish for her ruin, the Sant does not respond in kind. It is in this sense that the Sant is without enemies. The Sant does not respond with hate to those who hate. The Sant does not have an enemy mentality towards others. In a well-known Hindu prayer, offered before the flame of a lamp representing the Divine light, we pray for the blessings of prosperity and good health; but we also pray for the blessings of overcoming the enemy mentality (*shatru buddhi*) in our hearts.

> *Shubham karoti kalyanam*
> *arogyam dhana sampada*
>
> *Shatru buddhi vinashaya*
> *dipa jyotir namostute*
>
> I bow before the light of the Divine
> as I seek the blessings of wholeness,
> health, prosperity, and freedom
> from the enemy mentality.

This longing to be free from the enemy mentality is not unique to Hinduism. For example, it finds resonance in the Jewish tradition, in the story of Rabbi Meir and his wife Beruriah, which beautifully illustrates the transformation from wishing harm upon one's enemies to praying for their awakening.

> Rabbi Meir, a revered teacher,
> endured great hostility from some

of his neighbors. They slandered him, mocked him, and sought to harm him. Overcome by their cruelty, Rabbi Meir began to pray that they would die, so that his suffering would cease. His wife, Beruriah, a woman of great wisdom, listened to his prayers and gently corrected him. "Why pray for their death?" she asked. "Pray instead that they may turn from their malice. Do not pray for their destruction, but for their repentance." Moved by her words, Rabbi Meir changed his prayer, asking not for his enemies' downfall, but for their transformation. In time, the story tells us, they repented, and their hostility ended.

Here we see an ethic close to the Sant's freedom from the enemy mentality. To wish for the death of one's enemies is to be trapped in the cycle of hate. To wish instead for their transformation is to see beyond their actions and to recognize their deeper humanity. The Sant, like Rabbi Meir, resists responding to hate with hate. He hopes for the awakening of those caught in ignorance and extends compassion even to those who wish him harm.

How does one overcome the enemy mentality? In what follows, I offer a few suggestions.

First, we can practice seeing the Divine in everyone. When we are consumed by hate for another, we usually see nothing that is worthy of respect in them. In fact, we tend to dehumanize the other, and to see the individual other, or members of a group, in an entirely negative light. We deny anything good and worthy. At the heart of the Hindu tradition, however, is the core and definitive teaching that I always emphasize in my writings and lectures—that the Divine exists equally in everyone and in everything. Every sacred text that enunciates this teaching makes no exception. Despite the evil-doer being tragically unaware of the all-pervasive Divinity, evil conduct in human beings does not dispel the Divine reality present in the hearts of all. It is ignorance on our part if we fail to see the Divine in everyone.

One of the great dangers of hate is that it blinds us to seeing Divinity in others. Even when we must disapprove, resist, and condemn the evil conduct of another, we should not fail to see the Divine reality that is always present, clouded as it may be by thick layers of ignorance. Seeing in this way helps to free us from the enemy mentality.

Tulsidas gives us a striking example of this radical respect in the opening verses of his Ramayana. "I greet with a sincere heart," writes

Tulsidas, "the malevolent class, who are hostile without purpose even to the friendly, to whom others' loss is their own gain, and who delight in others' desolation and wail over their prosperity." He is not naïve about their evil characteristics and the pain that they inflict on others—yet he remarkably expresses his respect. In them, he sees his beloved Divine Rama. We see here that respect does not overlook the harm caused by those who act in ignorance.

Second, we can practice recognizing our shared identity. Hindu teachings understand the Divine as the very ground of the sense of self, and in that sense as the true Self (*atman*), Hindu texts speak interchangeably of seeing the Divine in all and seeing oneself in all. The sense of "I" is present only because of the ever-shining Divine Self. We are invited to know and to see ourselves in all beings and, as we have seen earlier, to regard their joy and sorrow as our own.

In order to hate and despise others, we always make the argument, in one form or another, that members of the despised community are different from us; we do not share anything with them. Hate and violence between one group and another require the denial of any shared identity. One way to counteract hate, violence, and injustice towards others is to understand our unity and shared identity with them. We exist in the same infinite

Divine who exists equally in every being. Since this one Divine exists as the deepest Self of all, we see ourselves in everyone, and we understand that to hate another is to hate oneself. Such seeing helps to liberate us from the enemy mentality.

Mahatma Gandhi, one of the great advocates of this teaching, wrote in his autobiography about its meaning for him:

> Man and his deed are two distinct things. Whereas a good deed should call forth approbation and a wicked deed disapprobation, the doer of the deed, whether good or wicked, always deserves respect or pity as the case may be. "Hate the sin and not the sinner" is a precept which, though easy enough to understand, is rarely practiced, and that is why the poison of hatred spreads in the world.

Third, we can practice seeing ignorance (*avidya*) as the root-cause of all evil. The way of *avidya*, ultimately ends in suffering and unhappiness, personal and social. In the Hindu tradition, we account for evil not with the argument that human nature is fundamentally flawed, but by tracing evil to *avidya* (ignorance) about the nature of reality,

God, universe, and humanity. *Avidya* leads to greed and greedful desires. Greedful desires generate actions that destroy self and others. Our attitude to the person caught in the grip of ignorance and who performs evil actions ought to be one of compassion and not hate.

Seeing *avidya* as the root cause of evil invites us to look deeper into the causes of another's conduct. Looking deeper helps us neutralize hate. A person who intentionally tells false and negative stories about you may be doing so out of envy for your success. He wants your achievements, but finds these difficult to attain. His frustration expresses itself in the desire to undermine you in the eyes of others by creating damaging stories. Understanding the cause of his behavior as his own inability to achieve success, enables you to control your own reaction of anger and hostility. You see the person's behavior as a product of his own predicament, and not something for which you are responsible or could control. You see it as a consequence of his own life's disappointments. It does not justify the person's actions, but it helps to liberate you from hate. The reasons why others may hate us are complex, and we cannot change them all in spite of our best efforts.

Our human tendency, however, is usually to react to the immediate word or action, and to become personally offended. We then want to hurt the other in the same manner that we are hurt, and we become entangled in a web of mutual animosity. In order to look beyond the word and action to the underlying causes, we must break this impulsive way of reacting and become more thoughtful and mindful in our responses. Although we are not responsible for the conduct of the other, we are responsible for our own thoughts, words, and actions, and can exercise control over these. Understanding the root cause of the other's actions helps us to better control our thoughts and actions. It does not make the behavior of the other correct or imply that the other is not responsible.

An attitude of understanding the cause of an action ensures that in any situation where another behaves disagreeably, we do not behave the same way. We instead respond on the basis of our own deeply held values. The ability to be in control of one's response, to deal justly with those who treat us unjustly, to love those who hate us, and to speak truth in the face of falsehood are the distinguishing characteristics of the Sant.

Freedom from the enemy attitude is not weakness, but an expression of wisdom. It does not mean approving of bad behavior or absolving people from responsibility, or that we should not protest against that which we consider to be unjust and a source of oppression and suffering. It means that we find a way to resist without hate in our hearts. If we can do so, we can be clearer about the reasons for our resistance. Gandhi and King, discussed earlier, were not perfect human beings, but they aspired to resist injustice without the enemy attitude (*abhutaripu*), and thus kept open the doors to reconciliation and peace.

Tulsidas prefaces his description of the Sant as free from the enemy attitude with the word "*sama,*" which means "same, equal or evenness of mind." It does not mean that the Sant is incapable of distinguishing someone who is friendly from someone who hates and is hostile. The Sant may indeed prefer the company of a friend over that of an enemy. What it means is that the Sant does not switch from an attitude of friendliness in the company of one who is a friend to one of hate when in the company of one who is unfriendly. The presence of hate does not radically alter the disposition of the Sant. The Sant is free from the enemy mentality.

4

TENDERHEARTED AND COMPASSIONATE TO THE POOR

Komalachita dinanha para daya

Tenderhearted and Compassionate to the Poor

Tulsidas, *Uttarakanda*

In Chapter 3, we discussed the Sant as one without enemies (*sama abhutaripu*). Others may regard and treat the Sant as their enemy, but the Sant does not consider anyone as an enemy. The Sant is free from the enemy mentality. Freedom from the enemy attitude is not weakness, but an expression of wisdom. It does not mean approving of harmful conduct or absolving people from responsibility, or never resisting or protesting against that which we consider to be unjust and a source of oppression and suffering. It means learning to resist without hate in our hearts. If we can do so, we can be clearer about the moral principles that guide our actions.

In this chapter, I invite you to consider a fourth virtue of the Sant, described by Tulsidas as being "tenderhearted and compassionate to the poor" (*komalchita dinanha para daya*). In Chapter 2, we discussed the Sant as empathizing with others in sorrow and in joy. Here, Tulsidas teaches that the compassion of the Sant is focused in a special way on those who are poor.

This concern was not abstract for Tulsidas; it arose out of his own early experience of poverty. His biographers describe him as an orphan growing up in and witnessing poverty. In the Ramayana, he describes poverty as the cause of the greatest suffering (*nahi daridra sama dukkha*). In fact, Tulsidas envisions the ideal society, *Ramrajya* (the kingdom of God), as one where such poverty and suffering are completely absent. In his vision of the ideal human society no one is poor, and all enjoy good health, are learned, and committed to each other's wellbeing. It is a community free from hate and violence. Centuries later, Gandhi drew deeply on this same vision of *Ramrajya* to articulate his own hope for a just society.

Extreme poverty is defined by the United Nations as "a condition characterized by severe deprivation of basic human needs, including food, safe drinking water, sanitation facilities, health, shelter, education and information. It depends not only on income but also on access to services." It is estimated that over one billion of our fellow human beings live in poverty, mainly in the developing countries, and more than a half of the world's poor are children. Poverty is a global challenge, and the Sant reminds us that we must be concerned.

The Hindu tradition recognizes the problem of poverty by including wealth (*artha*) as a goal necessary for human wellbeing. By including wealth as one of life's four goals, Hinduism recognizes that every human needs access to material necessities, such as food, education, healthcare, shelter, and clothing, that make life possible, and that enable human beings to live with dignity. Hinduism is not anti-materialistic; it is anti-greed and anti-selfishness.

In addition to *artha*, the other three goals are those of *kama* (pleasure), *dharma* (ethics), and *moksha* (liberation). *Kama* reminds us that the good life is not one reduced to the ascetic minimum. Life would be unattractive without the joys that we derive from music, song, dance, art, sports, good food, friends, and family. *Dharma* reminds us that wealth and pleasure must not be sought in ways that cause pain to others. We must always be cognizant of the common good and the wellbeing of others. We are social beings living in an interrelated world, and we cannot pursue our individual goals in life, such as wealth and pleasure, without regard for the happiness of others. Lastly, *moksha* underlines the necessity of spirituality for human fulfillment.

Swami Vivekananda (1863-1902), one of the most famous Hindu teachers in recent times, coined the expression *daridra narayana* (God as the poor). His intent was to appeal to Hindus to see God in the poor, and he equated the service of the poor with the true worship of God. "He who sees Shiva in the poor," said Vivekananda, "in the weak and in the diseased, really worships Shiva; and if he sees Shiva only in the image, his worship is but preliminary." Vivekananda's concept of *daridra narayana* enriches Tulsidas' description of the Sant as being compassionate to the poor. Vivekananda asks us to see and to serve God who is present as the poor.

I consider it relevant to our discussion on poverty that in traditional Hindu worship *(puja)*, we make a series of sixteen hospitality offerings to God. These include the invitation to receive worship, a seat, the washing of the feet, and acts of adoration through the offering of flowers, incense, food, clothing, water, and the waving of lights *(arati)*. Each offering is done mindfully and accompanied by the recitation of sacred words *(mantras)*, with a consciousness of the Divine being present and graciously receiving each offering.

The hospitality offerings include several that are essential for life and needed to overcome poverty. In the case of God, who has no need for our material offerings, these express our honor and reverence. In the case of the poor, however, food, water, shelter, and clothing are vital for survival. Vivekananda reminds us that we must not ignore the needs of God in human form; and furthermore, that if we offer these items to the poor with the consciousness that we are serving God who exists in the poor, our service becomes a mode of true worship.

The call to compassion for the poor and suffering is not unique to the Hindu tradition. In the Christian gospels, Jesus tells a parable that has inspired generations.

> A man was attacked by robbers on a lonely road, beaten, and left half-dead. A priest passed by, but offered no help. A Levite, one responsible for sacred duties, also saw the man and walked away. Then came a Samaritan, a member of a community despised and treated as outsiders. He was moved with compassion. Kneeling beside the

man, he bound his wounds with oil
and wine, placed him on his own
animal, and took him to an inn
where he could rest and recover.

The story of the Good Samaritan invites us to
see the heart of compassion in one who had no
obligation to help, and, indeed, every reason to
turn away. It reminds us that true spirituality is not
measured by ritual duty or religious identity, but by
tenderness toward the suffering. The story echoes
the Sant's compassion for the poor—the goodness
of the heart that transcends boundaries of class,
religion, or ethnicity, and sees, in every wounded
stranger, the face of God.

Much later, in 1968, Roman Catholic theology
spoke of "the preferential option for the poor,"
denoting a special obligation to care for the poor
and the vulnerable. This phrase became a part of
Catholic social teaching and a central tenet of what
we know as liberation theology.

Rabindranath Tagore (1861-1941), the Indian
poet and Nobel Prize winner, meditated on this
theme in one of his poems in *Gitanjali* (Song
Offering), the collection for which he received the
Nobel Prize.

Leave this chanting and
singing and telling of beads!

Whom dost thou worship
in this lonely dark corner of
a temple with doors all shut?

Open thine eyes and see thy
God is not before thee!

He is there where the tiller is
tilling the hard ground and where
the path-maker is breaking stones.

He is with them in sun and
in shower, and his garment
is covered with dust.

Put off thy holy mantle
and even like him come
down on the dusty soil!

Deliverance?

Where is this deliverance
to be found?

Our master himself has
joyfully taken upon him
the bonds of creation; he is
bound with us all forever.

Come out of thy meditations and
leave aside thy flowers and incense!

What harm is there if thy clothes
become tattered and stained?

Meet him and stand by him in
toil and in sweat of thy brow.

How does the Sant's compassion for the
poor speak to us? Minimally, the Sant reminds
us that we cannot be indifferent to poverty in
our communities, our nations, and our world. If
we understand wealth, as we do in Hinduism, as
essential for the good life, and if we are awake to
Divinity in all beings, we must care about those
who suffer. It is terribly wrong to think, as too
many do, that all people who are poor are so only
because they do not work hard enough. There
are so many reasons, historical and structural,
why large numbers of people live in poverty and
find it difficult to break out of the poverty cycle.
Working to overcome suffering means identifying
those political, social, and economic structures that
cause and perpetuate suffering. To blame the poor
for poverty is cruel and unjust.

In a similar way, it is immoral to justify
indifference to poverty by citing Hindu teachings
about *karma,* and arguing that poverty is a
consequence of immoral actions in past lives
and should, therefore, be seen as a form of just
punishment. Such a view ignores the most obvious
causes of poverty before our eyes. These include
historical injustices and exploitation that make

it difficult for large numbers of people across the world to overcome poverty.

Poverty is rooted in systemic structures such as race, caste, and even place of birth. Indifference to poverty also overlooks the consistent teachings in Hinduism to be generous and compassionate and to work for the overcoming of suffering. Fatalistic interpretations of *karma* paralyze our innate capacity for moral choice and action in service to the poor.

It is very important to take note of the fact that the Sant's concern for the poor is rooted in compassion. The Sant is tenderhearted and moved by suffering. Why is this significant? The economist, Jeffrey Sachs, in his book *The End of Poverty: Economic Possibilities for our Time* argues powerfully that the world has the resources to solve the problem of global poverty. What the world lacks, according to Sachs, is the will to do so.

For me, the absence of that will to act signifies the absence of care. It is the problem of indifference. The leadership of the developed countries is not moved enough by the plight of the poor, and the ideology of national insularity grows increasingly. We do not see ourselves in the poor. I believe that the work to overcome poverty that springs from love will be more enduring. Of course, it is consistent with and expresses the call of the Sant to identify with, and to see ourselves in, those who suffer. For the Sant, the root of social justice is love.

The Sant reminds us that changing the world also requires self-transformation. If one cause of the persistence of poverty is greed and a lack of care for those who suffer, the solution must also include inward human transformation, so that we become less greedy and more caring. This is why spirituality in the work of justice becomes important. Gandhi is often quoted as saying, "Be the change you want to see in the world." It is doubtful that Gandhi actually spoke these words, but their call to personal transformation is nonetheless powerful. Spiritually, the personal and the social are inseparable.

The Sant's concern for the poor invites us to become more generous and find ways to share with those in need. If we are active in temples and religious organizations, we must ensure that our temples are not just places for ritual worship and the celebration of festivals, but places of service for overcoming poverty. It may be as simple as a food shelf, or donating regularly to food shelves and places that distribute clothing and medicine. We must see this work as worship.

We must individually, and as members of religious congregations, support organizations working to address poverty. Here in the United States, there are many such organizations. Dr. William Barber, for instance, leads an interfaith effort, "The Poor People's Campaign," to highlight the problem of poverty in the United States and to encourage policies that address poverty. Caring for the poor is caring for the most vulnerable among us.

Finally, if we are concerned about poverty, we cannot be indifferent to politics, since state policies are important for the transformation of structures that perpetuate poverty. Gandhi reminded us of this when he wrote,

> To see the universal and all-pervading Spirit of Truth face to face, one must be able to love the meanest of creation as oneself. And a man who aspires after that cannot afford to keep out of any field of life. That is why my devotion to Truth has drawn me into the field of politics; and I can say without the slightest hesitation, and yet in all humility, that those who say that religion has nothing to do with politics do not know what religion means.

Gandhi was speaking of the need to bring the virtues of care and compassion to governmental policies. The moral virtues that he brought to his politics earned him the title of "*Mahatma*" (Great

Soul), but he could be equally described as a Sant
in his concern and work for the poor.

5

SUFFERING FOR THE SAKE OF OTHERS

Santa sahahim dukha parahita lagi

Endures Suffering for the Well-being of Others

Tulsidas, *Uttarakanda*

In Chapter 4, we took up the description of the Sant as one who is tenderhearted, compassionate, and generous to the poor. The Sant cares for all beings who suffer, but is concerned in a special way for the poor. I drew attention to Swami Vivekananda's description of the poor as *daridra narayana* (God as the poor) to call attention to the special claims of the poor on our attention and resources. Vivekananda appealed to us to see God in the poor and equated the service of the poor with the worship of God.

In this chapter, I invite you to consider a fifth virtue of the Sant. We have seen that the Sant empathizes with those who suffer. This gives rise to several questions. To what extent will a Sant work to help those who suffer? Is it only when it is convenient? Is it only when the Sant himself does not experience suffering? Tulsidas answers these questions by telling us that the Sant willingly endures suffering for the sake of freeing others from suffering. The Sant is not deterred by the risk of personal suffering.

Using an example from the natural world, as he loves to do, Tulsidas compares the Sant to the birch tree that allows its bark to be peeled away for the good of others. In earlier times, the bark was used as paper, and also for medicinal purposes, as it is believed to have analgesic properties. Those without virtue (*Asant*), on the other hand, are like the hemp plant that is used for making ropes to bind others and deprive them of freedom. The Asant will suffer to inflict pain on others. The Sant's suffering, in contrast, has a noble and higher purpose.

The Story of Rantideva

Let us turn now to a scriptural story that beautifully illustrates this virtue of enduring suffering for the sake of others. The Bhagavatam tells the story of Rantideva who was a poor and generous man, whose family faced many hardships because of their generosity. One morning, after going many days with little to eat or drink, they prepared a meager meal with what was available. Just as they were about to eat, a priestly guest arrived at their door. Remembering the teaching that God is present in everyone, Rantideva received his guest with respect and faith and shared a portion of the food. The priest, after eating, departed.

Rantideva divided the remaining food with his family, and was about to eat when another guest, a member of a lower caste, arrived. Remembering God, Rantideva also gave him a share of the food. After his guest left, a third guest arrived with dogs, saying, "O King, I and my dogs are hungry; please feed us." Rantideva, received them too with honor and respect, offering the food that remained to the dogs and their master.

Now, just the drinking water remained, and only enough to satisfy the thirst of one person. As Rantideva was about to drink, an untouchable appeared and said, "I am lowborn; give me some water." Hearing the touching words of the exhausted untouchable, Rantideva, moved with compassion, spoke these beautiful words:

> *I do not pray to God for the eight*
> *supernatural powers or for freedom*

from rebirth. I want to stay among
all living beings and share their
suffering, so that they may be free
from suffering.

In this profound prayer, Rantideva articulated a different understanding of the religious life that centers on compassion. He turned away from spirituality as a search for power, represented here by the aspiration for supernatural power, and from liberation construed as longing for freedom from the cycle of birth, death, and rebirth. In the place of power and freedom from rebirth, Rantideva prays for the opportunity to share the suffering of others so that they may be free from suffering. Rantideva's prayer is the Sant's prayer, and exemplifies that the highest ethical fruit of the religious life is compassion.

Hundreds of years later, in 1897, Swami Vivekananda would echo this aspiration in his famous words:

May I be born again and again and
suffer thousands of miseries so that
I may worship the only God that
exists, the only God I believe in, the
sum total of all souls—and above
all, my God the wicked, my God
the miserable, my God the poor of

all races, of all species, is the special
object of my worship.

Here also, Vivekanda regards compassion
and suffering for the sake of others as higher than
freedom from rebirth.

The Story of the Mongoose

Another traditional story, told in the
Mahabharata, offers a profound contrast between
external ritual and inner sacrifice. The story
recounts how Yudhisthira, after a great war, was
crowned king of Hastinapur. To celebrate his
victory and bring prosperity to his kingdom, he
wished to perform a grand religious ceremony.
After the very elaborate and expensive ceremony,
his subjects praised him for the best religious event
they had ever witnessed.

As the praises were showered on him, King
Yudhisthira noted a very strange phenomenon—a
mongoose, with half of its body golden and another
half brown, was rolling on the earth and looking
closely at its body. The gathering was puzzled and
stunned by this strange occurrence. Even more
astonishing was when the tiny mongoose then
spoke, and said, "There was nothing impressive
about your grand ritual, Yudhisthira; it was all just

a public show." Pained by this harsh judgement, the king asked the mongoose for an explanation.

"Many years ago," began the mongoose, "a poor man and his family, who were pious and generous, lived in a village. Once a great famine struck the village and everyone suffered. With great effort, the man procured a small amount of rice and divided it into four portions for his family. As they sat down to eat the tiny morsels, someone knocked on the door. A starving traveler, dying of hunger and thirst, lay on the ground. Immediately bringing him inside, the man offered his share. But after eating his modest portion, the traveler's hunger was not appeased; so each family member, in turn, offered him their share." As the mongoose recounted his tale, everyone listened in silence and rapt attention.

The mongoose continued his explanation: "Soon after, I happened to be passing by the house of that poor family, searching for food. In my scavenging, I accidentally touched a tiny bit of food that had remained on the dirt floor. To my amazement, half of my body turned golden! Since then, I have been traveling to religious ceremonies hoping to have the remaining half of my body made gold from contact with exemplary virtue. But as you can see, Yudhisthira, even though you gave away expensive gifts to everyone, your ritual was not as powerfully virtuous as the sacrifice of the poor family." And with these concluding words, the mongoose disappeared from the assembly, leaving everyone mystified.

The Story of Guru Hargobind in Sikhism

We may also learn from the Sikh tradition, where the life of Guru Hargobind reflects the same spirit of self-giving. Guru Hargobind was imprisoned by the Mughal emperor Jehangir, who feared his rising popularity and influence. Under pressure from moderate members of his community, Emperor Jehangir agreed to release him. Guru Hargobind, however, refused to accept his freedom unless the emperor also released the detained Hindu leaders, of which there were fifty-two. Jehangir insisted that only those who could hold on to the Guru's coattail would be freed. So Guru Hargobind arranged for a special coat, with fifty-two coattails, to be made, and walked out of the prison with all the Hindu leaders clutching the tassels of his coat! According to Sikh tradition, Guru Hargobind arrived at Amritsar, the sacred center of Sikhism, on Diwali day, and the city was illumined with thousands of earthen lamps to welcome him. He is celebrated for seeing his own freedom as inseparable from that of others and risking his freedom so that others would enjoy freedom.

—

Both the *Bhagavadgita* and the *Taittiriya Upanishad* provide specific moral guidelines for generosity. We must give with respect for the receiver of our gifts, not with disrespect that undermines the receiver's dignity. We must give joyfully in plenty, never with regret and always wishing that we could give more. We must give because it is good to give, and always without hope of reward. Generosity is not transactional. We must give at the right time, in the proper place, and to the neediest receiver.

According to Tulsidas, it is the Sant's natural disposition to serve others, even when such service involves personal risk. The Sant exemplifies a harmony and integrity at the three levels of thought, word, and action. These three energies are not pulling apart centrifugally, but flowing together centripetally. The Sant's effortless goodness is not unlike the love of a parent who would, without hesitation, rush out into a busy street to save her child who chased after a ball. Such integration does not happen overnight, since we all experience times when our thoughts, words, and actions are not in alignment. We may speak words and perform actions that, in our better moral moments, we know to be wrong.

The Sama Veda advises that if we know that caring for others is good, but we do not have caring thoughts in our heart, we should still act with care; we cannot wait until we have caring thoughts. The outward act of generosity gradually transforms our inward state and we become generous. The inward state does inform our outward actions, but the insight of the Veda is that outward actions also aid in transforming us inwardly.

The harmony of thought, word, and action is referred to in Hinduism as *trikarana shuddhi* (the purity of the three instruments). Although there are many techniques for fostering this integration, mindfulness and self-inquiry *(svadhyaya)* are primary ones. It is important that we reflect daily on our thoughts, our words, and our actions, to discern where these may not be in alignment and to return to coherence. It is also important that we remind ourselves each day of our aspiration for this integration. This may take the form of a morning prayer or practice to ground ourselves in our primary virtues and our commitment to express these consistently in our relationships. Daily grounding in prayerful practice and mindfulness are essential for the harmonizing of thought, words, and actions.

There is no greater gift of love than the willingness to suffer for another's sake. It is an ideal that must inspire our journey, even when the destination always seems far. For those of us seeking to cultivate virtue, but always falling short of our ideals, this beautiful verse can serve as a source of great encouragement:

> *In this effort, there is no loss.*
> *Small steps of practice are fruitful and*
> *save us from great fear.*

Bhagavadgita 2:40

6

Honoring All Beings

Sabahi manprada apu amani

Giving honor to all without demanding honor

Tulsidas, *Uttarakanda*

In Chapter 5, we reflected on the extent to which a Sant will go in trying to alleviate another's suffering. We looked at how Tulsidas likened the Sant to the birch tree that allows its bark to be stripped for the making of paper and medicines, and saw that the Sant does not shun the risk of personal suffering in serving others.

In this chapter, I invite you to consider a sixth virtue of the Sant, that of embodying humility. It is expressed by Tulsidas in the phrase, "Giving honor to all beings without demanding honor (*sabahi manprada apu amani*)."

The honor given by the Sant to others is inclusive. Tulsidas' wording is careful. He uses the word "*saba*," which excludes no one on the basis of age, gender, religion, ethnicity, or nationality. Extending honor to all human beings is a virtue dear to the heart of Tulsidas. In fact, he begins his composition on the life of Rama on this theme:

> *Eight million four hundred*
> *thousand species of living beings,*
> *classified under four broad*
> *divisions, inhabit land, water,*
> *and air. Realizing the whole*
> *world to be pervaded by Sita and*
> *Rama, I bow with folded hands.*

Tulsidas, *Balakanda*

In these lines, taken from the first chapter of the Ramayana, Tulsidas' statement about the number and variety of living beings is not meant to be a scientific statement for query and dispute. His intention is to draw our attention to the astonishing and rich biodiversity of our planet. Although we may never know the unique details of each life form, we do know the most important religious truth about life—all have come from God, and God exists in all. The value of the human being comes from the fact of this Divine origin and immanence, and not from wealth, profession, religion, gender, race, or language. Tulsidas expresses his own value for all beings when he describes himself as bowing before all beings with folded hands.

In his telling of the meeting between Rama and the forest-dweller Shabari, Tulsidas offers us a luminous example of honoring all beings. Here, the Divine himself reveals what it means to honor all.

> In the *Ramcharitmanas*, we hear of Shabari, a woman of low caste who lived in the forest, and longed for the day when Rama would visit her small ashram. Each morning she would gather fruits and berries, tasting each one first to be sure it was sweet, and set them aside for Rama. When Rama, accompanied by Lakshmana, finally came, he entered her humble dwelling without hesitation. Shabari fell at his feet, overwhelmed with devotion, and offered him the fruits she had carefully prepared. Rama received them with delight, eating each one joyfully.

In honoring Shabari's love, Rama broke the barriers of caste, poverty, and gender. He showed that what matters is not wealth or social status, but sincerity of heart. In honoring Shabari, Rama affirmed the Divine presence in every person, teaching us that to honor all beings is to honor God who dwells equally in all.

The existence of the Divine in everyone is the source of the intrinsic dignity of every being and the reason that honor is accorded to all. We cannot honor the Divine and dishonor the forms in which the Divine exists.

The Sant is able to honor all, because honor does not depend on the status of an individual or what an individual does or owns. If we honor on the basis of wealth, we exclude those who are not wealthy. If we honor on the basis of power, we will not honor the powerless. If we honor on the basis of religion, we will not honor those who do not belong to the religion we favor. If we privilege race, then we will exclude those who come from different races. If we practice caste, we will honor only those the caste system deems honorable. If we honor on the basis of nationality, we will value only those who belong to our nation. When we honor on the basis that the Divine exists equally in all beings, then we cannot exclude anyone. Honor is given because of the intrinsic nature of every being. I cannot emphasize this enough.

The Sant is *amani,* one who is humble and honors all. For the *mani,* the person who is the opposite of the Sant, honor and respect are diminishing values. By a diminishing value, I mean the belief that honor is a finite sum; when honor is accorded to one person, there is less to be given to another. For the *mani,* who constantly demands respect from others, respect given to another diminishes what is given to him. For this reason, *manis* are unlikely to honor others, and are uncomfortable when others are honored. They wish for the light of honor to shine exclusively on them.

The *mani* is not only ignorant of the Divine reality present in others, but also unaware of the Divinity dwelling in his own heart. At a fundamental level, the *mani* lacks intrinsic self-value, and expresses this in a lack of value for others. To know God as present in all is to know God as present in oneself, and to respect and value oneself and others accordingly.

Let me emphasize again that treating others with respect and honor does not require always agreeing with everything they say or do or never being critical of choices that they make. What it means is that when a Sant disagrees with another or has to oppose another, the Sant does so without contempt, denigration, or abuse. To be a Sant is to know how to oppose and to disagree honorably, with self-respect and with respect for the other. The virtues of the Sant are born of strength, not weakness.

"We as a society have not learned," said Martin Luther King Jr., "to disagree without being violently disagreeable." In our public life, we witness, regrettably, the increasing failure to express differences with respect and honor for others. We seem to think that mockery and denigration are signs of strong and confident leadership, setting a poor example for our children. In this regard, we have much to learn from the way of the Sant.

The sentence of Tulsidas under discussion here has two parts. He first speaks of the Sant as giving honor to all beings (*sabahi manprada*), and then notes that the Sant does not demand honor from others (*apu amani*). A *mani*, unlike the Sant, has an exaggerated sense of self-importance and always demands honor from others. The Sant is *amani* and makes no such demands.

This ideal of equanimity is also praised in the thirteenth chapter of the *Bhagavadgita*, which enumerates a list of virtues that express spirituality. Interestingly, the first virtue mentioned is freedom from an exaggerated sense of self-importance (*amanitvam*).

Why is a Sant free from the obsession for honor? He or she understands that respect is meaningful only when it is freely given because others discern something worthy of respect. Even as one cannot command love, one cannot command respect. Those who speak of demanding respect do not understand the nature of respect. It is appropriate to demand equality before the law and rights accorded to others. Honor, however, is different.

Demand for respect easily leads to flattery. A person who demands respect will often receive empty gestures of respect. In his presence, people may act respectfully and speak words of praise; but such gestures and accompanying words will always lack sincerity of heart. These may be motivated by fear of the other's anger and ability to hurt them. This is true of individuals, but can also be true of nations and states. The obsession with honor and greatness is a grave problem and a significant character flaw, especially in leaders.

The *mani,* who demands respect, creates an atmosphere of friction and tension. He is in tension because he is always scrutinizing others to ensure that he receives respect, and is quite easily offended if what he regards as proper respect is not given. People around a *mani* are in tension because they are terrified of offending him. This usually happens when a *mani* has the power to hurt or reward others.

The great paradox of the *mani* is that while he may assert his power and independence, he completely depends on others for a sense of wellbeing. There is a glaring contradiction here— the *mani* suffers from both an exaggerated sense of self-importance and a deep sense of self-doubt. For this reason, he needs constant validation from others to satisfy an insatiable inner lack.

The Sant does not invite others to dishonor him or enjoy disrespect. As a human being, a Sant appreciates honor and respect, but doesn't demand it or complain about its absence. He is gracious in accepting honor, and calm when it is not given.

Mahatma Gandhi spoke often of the example of a rose, which, I think, is appropriate here:

> *A rose does not need to preach.*
> *It simply spreads its fragrance.*
> *The fragrance is its own sermon.*

A rose, whether in a cultivated garden or growing in the wild, blooms in radiant color and emits its attractive fragrance; yet the rose does not boast of either its color or fragrance. Some may pause in appreciation, and others may not even notice its existence, but the rose does not wither if it goes unnoticed. Though the color and fragrance of religion and spiritual life is much finer and more subtle than that of a rose, the beauty of the rose is similar to that of the Sant's spiritual life. The Sant does not proclaim her spiritual virtues. Those who value the spiritual life may honor the Sant; many more may not. The Sant's way of being remains unaltered by praise or lack thereof.

Bhagavadgita 5:18, uses a very beautiful phrase, "rich in knowledge and humility *(vidya-vinaya-sampanne),*" to describe the person centered in the Divine. Where there is spiritual knowledge, there is always humility. The humility of the Sant is a consequence of gratitude. Whatever the spiritual virtues and accomplishments, the Sant recognizes his indebtedness to others. In our religious journeys, we all benefit from the guidance of our immediate teachers and from the lineage of teachers who have preserved and transmitted wisdom across the ages.

The truth of humility is also rooted in recognizing that our existence and flourishing depends on the universe and its complex network of interrelated beings. The Hindu tradition speaks of the human being as born with debts *(rna).* Although three of these are emphasized (God, teachers, and ancestors), the list includes the world of nature and all human beings. By acknowledging the truth of our constant indebtedness to others, known and unknown, we grow in humility and overcome our disposition toward false independence, arrogance, and craving honor. Although many speak of themselves and their success as "self-made," Hinduism reminds us of our reality as receivers dependent on the generosity of others. The proper response to being a receiver is gratitude and humility.

There is, however, a further point that needs to be made. Understanding our continuous indebtedness and the interdependent nature of our existence comes with the moral obligation to be generous givers. In the *Bhagavadgita* (3:12), the teacher, Krishna, describes the person who receives from others without giving back as a thief. He likens such a person to one who cooks only for himself. The virtuous person, on the other hand, always cooks for himself and for others. Knowing ourselves to be indebted demands grateful generosity.

This is the way of the Sant, whose humility leaves no room for the inextinguishable greed for praise and tribute from others.

7

TRANQUIL IN DEFAMATION AND PRAISE

Ninda astuti ubhaya sama

Tranquil in Defamation and Praise

Tulsidas, *Uttarakanda*

In Chapter 5, we discussed the Sant as one who treats every being with honor, but never demands honor from others. In relationships, the Sant embodies humility. He is gracious in accepting honor, but calm and balanced when it is not received.

In this chapter, I invite you to consider a seventh virtue of the Sant, described by Tulsidas in the phrase, *ninda astuti ubhaya sama* (tranquil in defamation and praise). *Ninda* is often translated as blame, but its meaning is much stronger, and closer to slander. *Ninda* is speech meant to denigrate, defame, and cause pain or harm. It is speech that belittles another in order to make one feel better about oneself. *Astuti*, on the other hand, are words of praise, commendation, and appreciation. In relation to both of these, the Sant is described as *sama*, which is often translated as "same." In some contexts, this meaning is appropriate, but, here, I prefer to translate *sama* as tranquil or calm. The meaning of the phrase then is that the Sant is calm when defamed or praised.

The *Bhagavadgita* (12:18-19; 14:24) also highlights this ability to stay calm in the face of praise or slander, reinforcing this as an important attribute of the Sant, the devotee *(bhakta)* and the wise person *(jñāni)*.

How is such a state possible? Do we not experience elation when we are praised and depression when denigrated? Do we not depend on words of praise from others for our sense of wellbeing? Is our sense of wellbeing not diminished when we are slandered? How does one remain calm, tranquil, and balanced amidst praise or slander?

The most important answer to these questions is that the Sant's inner wellbeing does not depend on receiving praise from others, and it is not shattered by denigration. The source of the Sant's wellbeing lies elsewhere. Where is it to be found?

The conclusion of the second chapter of the *Bhagavadgita* discusses the qualities and virtues of a person well-established in spiritual wisdom. Krishna describes this person as finding his or her contentment in the *atman*, the indwelling Divine reality that is full and whole and equally existent in all beings. It is here that the wise finds meaning, satisfaction, and delight. It is this rootedness, this centeredness in the *atman* and its nature of peace *(shantih)* and joy *(ananda)* that informs the Sant's response to praise and blame.

Now consider this—in the absence of this deep state of inward contentedness, we are more likely to become dependent on, or even addicted to, receiving words of praise from others for our wellbeing. We find our elation, our euphoria, our ecstasy in these words of praise, and experience an inward lack when such words are not forthcoming. People easily recognize our need and love for praise, and this makes us vulnerable and susceptible to flattery. We gravitate towards those who praise us, and we reward them. We become dependent on praise, and in its absence, we sink easily into dejection.

When we depend on praise for our sense of wellbeing, it follows logically that words of denigration hurt us even more deeply. These shatter our composure. If we love only those who praise us, we respond with hate towards those who denigrate and demean us. In this way, we are constantly riding an emotional rollercoaster of highs and lows, and we become completely dependent on others for our wellbeing.

In Chapter 2:70 of the *Bhagavadgita*, Krishna uses a beautiful analogy of the ocean. In the depths of the ocean, there is a stillness, a peace, which ripples on the surface do not reach. Even the raging rivers are peacefully absorbed in the ocean's fullness. In a similar way, the surface ripples of blame and praise do not upset the abiding peace in the Sant's heart. If we live only at the level of the ripples, our peace wavers and is transient. When we live at the depths, the ripples are just that—ripples on the surface.

There is an important clarification to be made here. We must not understand the calmness of the Sant to mean that he or she does not recognize the difference between praise and defamation and does not prefer one over the other. Of course, the Sant, like each of us, is able to tell the difference and prefers good and kind words over demeaning ones. The difference is that the Sant does not get attached to praise or enter a state of misery when the words are not favorable. Appreciating praise is one thing; being attached to and dependent on praise is entirely different.

A well-known Buddhist story provides a memorable example of this principle in action.

One day, the Buddha was traveling through a village. A very angry and rude young man approached and began insulting him, hurling all kinds of derogatory words intending to ridicule and demean him.

The Buddha was not upset by these insults. Instead, he questioned the young man, "Tell me, if you bring a gift for someone, and that person does not accept it, to whom does the gift belong?"

Though surprised to be asked such an unusual question, the young man answered, "It would belong to the person who brought the gift."

The Buddha calmly smiled and said, "That is correct. And it is exactly the same with your anger. If you become angry with me and I do not get insulted, then the anger stays with you. You are then the one who becomes unhappy, not me. All you have done is hurt yourself."

The point is that we are not under any obligation to accept the gifts of others, and especially those gifts that cause us to surrender our peace and composure to another. *Ninda* is such a gift: if it causes you to be miserable, you have accepted it; if not, it stays with the gift-giver.

Praise and fame are not wrong in themselves. When a Sant engages in action, he or she is not motivated by winning others' praise; it is service. If praise is not forthcoming, the Sant will not cease to work. If praise comes, he or she receives it with a calm and balanced mind. Praise, as is popularly said, does not go to the Sant's head.

Similarly, we must distinguish *ninda* from disagreement. A person who expresses a different opinion or offers a word of criticism is not engaging in *ninda*.

A disagreement, however, may very easily turn into *ninda*. When it does, it moves from being a difference of views, and becomes an attack on the humanity of the other that aims to undermine the other's self-worth. Those engaging in *ninda* are more likely to spread slanderous words.

It is problematic when disagreements degenerate into *ninda,* but it is also problematic when every disagreement or criticism is treated as *ninda*. Unfortunately, this is too often the case for many people who are not open to any kind of challenge or criticism. If we see disagreements as *ninda*, we are likely to malign those who disagree with us. *Bhagavadgita* 17:15 commends the discipline of words to avoid speech slipping into *ninda*. The text is quite explicit on this point:

Words that do not demean, and that are truthful, pleasant, beneficial, and consistent with scriptural teaching constitute disciplined speech.

Because of the Sant's secure sense of self-worth, located in self-knowledge, he is able to deal more objectively with *ninda* and to respond with control. The Sant is able to look beyond the *ninda* and to see that the problem is with the person's slanderous motivation.

There may be several reasons why people engage in *ninda*. They may be instigated by envy and the desire to hurt the reputation and hamper the success of someone whom they regard as a rival. *Ninda*, sadly, helps some to feel better about themselves, particularly those suffering from low self-esteem. Such a person hopes to rise in self-value by undermining the value of another. *Ninda* often gives those who share demeaning information about others a sense of power. They experience a feeling of satisfaction in having privileged information, even if the information shared is false. This also is born of low self-esteem.

Understanding such motivations, the Sant is able to maintain calmness, and does not respond with hate or seek revenge. Instead, the Sant maintains his composure, and looks deeper, beyond the person's action alone, to compassionately respond to the person themselves.

What about praise? While the Sant can certainly tell the difference between praise and defamation, and can prefer one over the other, the Sant knows that the motivations for words of praise can be quite varied. They may spring from a genuine place of respect and honor, but not always. Sometimes words of praise come from the fact that the person praised has power and the praiser expects benefit—if the praised loses power, the praise vanishes. Some people praise because they expect praise in return, and cease to praise when it is not reciprocated. Praise may be given as long as one advocates for a view that the other supports, but then withdrawn when one challenges the other's viewpoint.

The Sant does not reject praise, but understands clearly that it is unpredictable and fickle; praise given one day may be withdrawn on another. Regardless, the Sant abides in calmness (*sama*).

8

The Instrument of God in the World

Chandana taru hari santa samira

God is the sandal tree; the Sant is the wind

Tulsidas, *Uttarakanda*

In this journey of considering the virtues of the Sant together, we have arrived at the final chapter. The virtues of the Sant will not be exhausted in a single short discussion, but we have lifted up a few of the primary ones.

In Chapter 1, we explored how the Sant consistently manifests goodness even amidst hate and violence, like the sandal tree that gives its beautiful fragrance even to the axe that cuts it. In Chapter 2, we saw that the Sant empathizes with people in both joy and sorrow, and is never indifferent to the plight of others. In Chapter 3, we learned that the Sant is free from the enemy attitude; others may be hostile toward the Sant, but the Sant never hates in return. In Chapter 4, we turned to the Sant's special concern, generosity, and responsiveness toward the poor who suffer from lacking the necessities for decent living. In Chapter 5, the Sant's willingness to risk personal loss to lift others from suffering was highlighted. In Chapter 6, we saw that the Sant is humble, and gives honor to all beings without demanding honor for himself. In Chapter 7, we observed that the Sant's fullness and contentment are centered in the Divine reality existing in everyone's heart, enabling the Sant to remain remarkably calm amidst both praise and defamation.

In this final chapter, we turn to the nature of the Sant as the instrument and servant of the Divine in our world. The virtuous life of the Sant expresses the Sant's centeredness in the Divine reality. The Sant's goodness flows from the absolute goodness of God. If a cold object is placed directly in the sunshine, it absorbs the sun's warmth and radiates it to others. In a similar way, the Sant's heart is warmed by Divine goodness, and radiates outward as love and compassion.

Virtues do not always have to emerge from a place of religious commitment and meaning. Religious people do not have an exclusive claim on goodness, and are not the only ones committed to ethical conduct. But virtues can express religious commitment, and this is true in the case of the Sant. For Tulsidas, the person devoted to God is also devoted to the wellbeing of others, and, as we have noted throughout, is compassionate and empathizes with those who suffer. Similarly, *Bhagavadgita* 12:4 says that the lover of God rejoices in the flourishing of all beings. Virtues are a manifestation of the Sant's awakening to God, but also the stepping-stones on the path to God. The practice of virtue is both goal and way.

If the Sant's embodiment of virtue expresses his or her centeredness in God, how may we describe the Sant's role in relation to God? Tulsidas uses two beautiful metaphors, using his favorite name for God, Rama.

> Rama is the ocean; the virtuous are the rain clouds (*rama sindhu ghana sajjana dhira*).

> Rama is the sandal tree; the Sant is the wind (*chandana taru hari santa samira*).

As God is the source of all that exists, the ocean is the source of our life-giving water. Like Divinity, the ocean is deep, unfathomable, inexhaustible. When we stand on an ocean shore, we do so with a sense of awe and humility in the face of its vastness and mystery. It is the water of the ocean, in the form of rain, that nourishes the earth and sustains life in all its many forms.

Tulsidas clearly understood the phenomenon of weather. The energy of the sun causes water on the surface of the ocean to evaporate into water vapor. This vapor then rises into the atmosphere, where the air is colder, and condenses into clouds. Air currents then move these clouds around the globe.

We do not experience the blessings of the ocean without the instrumentality of the clouds, which make the ocean accessible by conveying its water to our fields, rivers, lakes, and wells. The clouds are the instruments of the ocean. In a similar way, Sants are instruments through whom we experience the reality and blessings of God in our lives. Like clouds absorbing water from the ocean and releasing it on earth, the Sant draws deeply from the Divine, the ocean of love and compassion, and expresses these qualities in his relationship with others. They are the visible manifestations of the invisible.

The sandal tree emits a beautiful fragrance, but it is the wind that spreads this perfume everywhere. It is wind that transports the molecules that enable us to smell anything. Sandalwood is the symbol of the beauty, grace, and peace that a good person embodies and shares with others. In the absence of clouds or the wind, we will not receive the water's blessing or the sandalwood's fragrance. We may even say that the ocean and the sandal tree depend on the clouds and the wind to accomplish their purposes in the world.

One of the beautiful dimensions of these examples is the beneficent nature of the clouds and wind. A cloud does not retain the ocean's water for its own purpose, but releases the nourishing water over the land, unselectively pouring its blessings on all. Similarly, the wind does not selfishly retain the fragrance of the sandal tree, but spreads it wherever it blows. Clouds and the wind do not discriminate. Likewise, the Sant serves as God's instrument for everyone and in all circumstances. Like the clouds or the wind, the Sant does not bless some and withhold blessings from others.

Good religion does not lead to being self-centered; it empowers and inspires us to become instruments of goodness in the world. How can we, like rain clouds, be life-giving and nourishing of others? How, like the fragrant wind, can we fill their lives with beauty and joy?

Clouds and winds are active. They move very far from their point of origin, sometimes crossing entire continents. Similarly, our religious lives cannot be confined to the walls of our homes, temples, and institutions. Our journey may start from these places, but ought not end there. We need to look beyond these walls to become, like the Sant, a servant of God in our community, nation, and world.

These two metaphors used by Tulsidas help us better understand the nature of Divine activity in the world, and the ways in which we experience the blessings of God. We too often think of God's blessings as intangible, and we may find it difficult to discern God's response to our prayer. We may think that the blessings of God come to us only in miraculous ways that run contrary to the laws of nature and are independent of the human community.

Tulsidas' words remind us that God enters into our lives, in a real way, through the actions of the virtuous. They are the instruments through which God's blessings pour into our lives. If we do not understand this, we may miss the many ways and moments we receive such blessings. Those who serve, comfort, and care for others manifest God's reality.

This way of being an instrument of God is not only expressed in lofty metaphors, but also in the very ordinary encounters of daily life. One of the most powerful examples comes from the life of St. Francis of Assisi, whose meeting with a leper became the turning point of his journey, and a luminous sign of what it means to serve as God's instrument in the world.

As a young man, Francis of Assisi avoided lepers, turning away in fear and revulsion. One day, however, as his heart was being drawn more deeply to God, he met a leper on the road. Though everything in him recoiled, Francis felt moved to dismount, place coins in the man's hand, and then, overcoming his disgust, bend down and kiss the leper's hand.

Francis later described this encounter as the moment his life was transformed. What once seemed bitter to him became sweet. In the face of the outcast, he encountered God, and his heart was opened to live as an instrument of God's love, especially among the poor, the sick, and the forgotten. In Francis's embrace of the leper, the fragrance of God's love was carried into the world—just as the wind bears the sweetness of sandalwood—transforming fear into tenderness and exclusion into embrace.

—

Some years ago, when the Covid pandemic swept across our world, many searched for God and asked "Where is God?" Tulsidas answers this question by directing our attention to the virtuous servants. God was active in the resolute, heroic, and vulnerable work of health care providers, who risked their lives each day to save the lives of others, and who, when they were unable to do more, whispered final words of comfort to the dying. God was active in ambulance drivers racing across cities, and in the emergency medical technicians who served as first responders to those who had fallen ill. God was active in the work of scientific researchers who, inspired by a passion for relieving suffering, left no stones unturned to find vaccines and curative therapies. The servant of God in the pandemic was anyone generously giving through the work of healing, comforting, and supporting others. The mark of God's presence is not a loud proclamation of oneself as a servant of God, but the humble outpouring of self in acts of loving service. In the pandemic, we affirmed and acknowledged God by what we did for others. If we know where to look, God is not absent. God's presence is limited only by the limits of our seeing.

Here is a short parable that captures how we sometimes overlook Divine help when it arrives through ordinary channels:

> One day, a man sitting in his home heard a loud explosion. He saw people running in panic from their homes, and discovered that a dam had burst. The river was flooding

the town and people were being evacuated. Noticing the water rising in the streets, he too felt a sense of panic, but decided that he would stay in his home and trust God to protect him. As the water reached his window, a boatful of people came by. "Jump in," they shouted. "No, no," he answered, "I trust in the providence of God to save me." As the water continued to rise, he moved to the top floor of his home. Another boatload of people came by and urged him to join them. Once again, he refused. The water continued to rise, and he moved to the roof. A member of the fire service was sent, on a motorboat, to rescue him. "No thank you," said the man. "I trust in God. He will not let me down." When he drowned and came before God, he complained noisily, "I trusted you! Why did you do nothing to save me?" "Well," said God, "I did send three boats and you turned them all away."

—

After sharing these two metaphors, Tulsidas adds that the fruit of all spiritual efforts is the awakening of love for God; this awakening, however, is the gift of the Sant. Even though we may not see the distant ocean, the clouds that originate in the ocean and the rain showers that replenish the earth attest to the ocean's reality. In a similar way, we may live far from the sandal tree, but the fragrant wind is evidence of its existence. The Sants, who live in our midst, committed to virtue, and willing to offer life itself for the love of others, are themselves powerful signs and testimony of God's reality. Their lives of love and compassion teach and reveal the nature of the Divine as limitless love and goodness.

Again, if we know where to look, God is not absent. God's presence is limited only by the limits of our seeing.

Let us conclude this reflection with the story of one such presence, Sant Bahinabhai, a woman in the tradition of the Sants, who lived in 17th-century Maharashtra. Her life offers a gentle, yet powerful, embodiment of what it means to be an instrument of God in the world.

> At a young age, Bahinabai was married off to a man who had no sympathy for her devotional aspirations. Her days were filled with labor—caring for the home, fetching water, grinding grain—all

the while navigating the loneliness of an unsupportive marriage. Yet, through every act of service, her heart remained quietly fixed on Vitthal, the Divine presence she felt everywhere. For Bahinabai, the water pot and the broom became sacred, her home became a temple. She attested to this reality, saying:

While I churn buttermilk,
I remember You.

While sweeping the courtyard,
I remember You.

You are present in the rice,
in the water, in the broom.

My God,
You have taken residence
in all things.

One morning, as she carried her pot of water home from the river, she encountered an old, frail woman by the roadside. Some villagers mocked her; others passed without care. Bahinabai knelt beside her and gave her the water she had just drawn. The woman drank, her voice

shaking with gratitude. Bahinabai
returned home with an empty pot
and a full heart, and penned these
words:

You sat there in rags, thirsty.
When I quenched Your thirst,
my hands were empty,
but my soul overflowed.

Bahinabai was not a renunciant in the
traditional sense. She lived in the world, but not
for herself. Her renunciation was inward—a
letting go of pride, resentment, and the desire for
recognition. Her spiritual strength was not forged
in retreat from life, but through gentle, daily acts
of compassion. She never called herself a Sant,
but her life emitted the fragrance of Divine love,
carried like sandalwood perfume on the wind of
her humility.

In Bahinabai, we see that the Sant is not always
a person of public stature. The Sant may live quietly,
unknown to the world, but known to God. She
exemplifies the cloud that brings the water of love,
the wind that carries God's grace into forgotten
corners. Her very being becomes prayer, her service
becomes presence. Seeing such lives reminds us that
God's work in the world is done not only through
great leaders, but also through quiet souls who

embody compassion in obscurity. The Sant is not a monument to be venerated from a distance, but a path to be followed—a way of seeing, serving, and loving in every season and circumstance.

CONCLUSION:
WALKING THE WAY OF THE SANT

Dear reader, I close this offering by reminding you that the way of the Sant is not a distant ideal reserved for the few, but an invitation for us all. Each virtue we have considered—gentleness like the sandal tree, empathy with others in sorrow and joy, freedom from the enemy mentality, compassion for the poor, willingness to suffer for others, honoring all beings, calm in praise and defamation, and serving as instruments of the Divine—forms part of a single path.

To walk this path is to let our hearts be shaped by love, to allow compassion to widen our vision, and to see the Divine shining in every being. It is to live each day with humility and courage, mindful that our smallest actions leave a fragrance in the lives of others.

We may falter and feel unworthy of so luminous a calling. Yet, as Tulsidas reminds us, even a chip of sandalwood carries its fragrance. Small acts of kindness, moments of forgiveness, and gestures of care are not insignificant; they are the seeds of a more compassionate world.

In honoring the Sants, we are reminded that holiness is not only found in temples or scriptures, but in the way we live with one another. The world longs for such fragrance, for lives that heal, reconcile, and uplift.

May we, in our own imperfect yet sincere ways, walk this path. May we learn to be sandalwood in a world of axes, winds that carry the Divine fragrance, and instruments through whom love is made visible.

With this prayer in our hearts, I will leave you with the following poem:

Sant Stuti: Ode to the Sant

The way of the Sant is a gentle path,
yet it asks of us great courage.
It is the courage to remain fragrant when struck,
to feel another's sorrow as our own,
to see no enemy even when others see one in us,
to bow before all beings with reverence.
It is the way of compassion for the poor,
the willingness to suffer
so that another may be freed,
the humility to honor without demanding honor,
the steadiness of heart in blame and in praise.
The Sant teaches us that holiness is not distant.
It is here—in the quiet act of kindness,

in the tender word spoken to one in pain,
in the unseen gesture of care that no one applauds.
Even a splinter of sandalwood carries its fragrance.
Even the smallest act of love lingers in the air.
The Sants remind us:
we need not be perfect to shine,
only faithful to the light that dwells within.
May we learn to walk gently,
leaving behind not bitterness, but fragrance;
not division, but peace;
not pride, but humility.
In this world of axes,
may we live as sandal trees,
may we breathe as the fragrant wind,
and may our lives whisper of the Divine
long after our voices are silent.

Bibliography

Bhagavadgita. Translated by Winthrop Sargeant. Albany: State University of New York Press, 1993.

The Upanishads. Translated by Patrick Olivelle. Oxford: Oxford University Press, 1996.

Tulsidas, *Sri Ramacaritamanasa*. Translated by R.C. Prasad. Delhi: Motilal Banarsidass, 1991.

GLOSSARY

Ahimsa

Nonviolence; the Sanskrit term meaning not to harm. More than mere absence of violence, it is an active expression of love and care for all beings.

Amani

One who is humble and does not demand honor from others. The Sant is described as *apu amani*—not obsessed with status or self-importance.

Artha

Wealth; one of the four goals of life in Hinduism, recognizing the importance of material wellbeing for a dignified life.

Asant

The opposite of a Sant; one who lacks virtue. Used by Tulsidas to contrast those who cause harm with those who live in love and service.

Astuti

Praise or commendation. The Sant is said to remain tranquil in both *ninda* (slander) and *astuti* (praise).

Atman

The Divine Self; the innermost essence that is present equally in all beings. It is identical with the Supreme Reality (Brahman) in many Hindu teachings.

Bhakta

A devotee or lover of God. In the Bhagavadgita, the *bhakta* is one who loves God and all beings.

Brahma veda brahmaiva bhavati

"He who knows Brahman (the Divine), becomes Brahman." A teaching from the Mundaka Upanishad expressing the transformative power of Divine knowledge.

Chandana

Sandalwood; often symbolizing purity, peace, and enduring goodness. The Sant is likened to a sandal tree that gives fragrance even to the axe that cuts it.

Daridra Narayana

Literally, "God as the poor." A term coined by Swami Vivekananda to emphasize service to the poor as a form of Divine worship.

Daya

Compassion. A central virtue in the Hindu tradition, especially embodied by the Sant.

Dharma

Ethical living, duty, or righteousness. One of the four goals of life, guiding the pursuit of wealth and pleasure within moral boundaries.

Dipajyoti

The flame of a lamp, often representing Divine light. In Hindu prayer, the lamp is revered as a symbol of auspiciousness and moral clarity.

Dvesha

Hatred or intense aversion. The Sant is free from *dvesha*, even toward those who act with hostility.

Gita / Bhagavadgita

A sacred Hindu scripture composed as a dialogue between Krishna and Arjuna. It explores themes of duty, devotion, and spiritual wisdom.

Hanuman

The devoted servant of Rama in the Ramayana, and an exemplar of love, courage, and service.

Jñāni

A person of knowledge, particularly spiritual knowledge. In the Gita, the *jñani* is one who abides in the Self and sees unity in all beings.

Kama

Pleasure; one of the four goals of life in Hinduism. It includes aesthetic, emotional, and sensory enjoyment.

Karma

Action and its moral consequences. Often misunderstood, karma in Hinduism reflects the law of cause and effect, not fatalism.

Komalachita

Tenderhearted; used by Tulsidas to describe the Sant's softness toward the poor and suffering.

Maha Upanishad

An ancient Hindu text which contains the well-known teaching *vasudhaiva kutumbakam*—"the whole world is one family."

Mahatma

"Great Soul"; a title often used for Gandhi, recognizing his spiritual and moral greatness.

Mani

A *mani* is someone obsessed with personal honor and recognition.

Moksha

Spiritual liberation or release from the cycle of rebirth. It is the highest of the four goals of life.

Ninda

Defamation or slander. Tulsidas contrasts *ninda* (denigration) with *astuti* (praise), highlighting the Sant's calm in both.

Para dukha dukhi

Sorrow in another's sorrow; a phrase from Tulsidas describing the Sant's empathy.

Puja

Worship ritual in Hinduism. Offerings include flowers, water, incense, food, and light to express reverence.

Ramacharitamanas

The retelling of the Ramayana by Tulsidas in the Awadhi language. It is a devotional epic highlighting the virtues of Rama and the Sants.

Rama

Divine person of the Ramayana, regarded as an incarnation of Vishnu. Central to the teachings of Tulsidas.

Ramrajya

The ideal kingdom or society envisioned by Tulsidas and Gandhi, based on justice, harmony, and care for all.

Rantideva

A noble character in the Bhagavatam who embodies generosity and prays to share in the suffering of others.

Samira

Wind. In a metaphor by Tulsidas, God is the sandal tree and the Sant is the wind spreading its fragrance.

Sama

Equanimity or balance. The Sant is *sama*—tranquil in blame and praise, friend and enemy.

Sant

Derived from *sat*, meaning truth or goodness. A virtuous being who embodies love, humility, and devotion.

Satyagraha

"Truth-force"; Gandhi's term for nonviolent resistance based on moral power and deep conviction.

Satyam eva jayate

"Truth alone triumphs." A verse from the Mundaka Upanishad and a foundational ideal in Indian ethics.

Shatru / Shatru Buddhi

Enemy / Enemy mentality. The Sant is free from *shatru buddhi*, even when others act as enemies.

Sita

Wife of Rama in the Ramayana; an icon of dignity, virtue, and devotion.

Svadhyaya

Self-study or self-reflection; a key practice in the cultivation of virtue and integrity.

Tulsidas

16th-century Hindu poet-saint and author of the
Ramacharitamanas.

Upanishads

Foundational Hindu philosophical texts that explore the
nature of ultimate reality, the self, and liberation.

Vasudhaiva kutumbakam

"The whole world is one family." A celebrated Hindu
teaching of universal kinship and compassion from the
Maha Upanishad.

Vidya-Vinaya-Sampanna

"Rich in knowledge and humility." A phrase from the Gita
describing the truly wise.

Sadguna

Virtue; a moral quality such as compassion, humility, or
honesty.

Yogi

One who practices yoga, especially in its broader sense of
disciplined spiritual living. The best *yogi*, according to the
Gita, sees the Self in all beings.

Anantanand Rambachan is Professor Emeritus of Religion at Saint Olaf College, Minnesota, USA.

His books include *Accomplishing the Accomplished: The Vedas as a Source of Valid Knowledge in Sankara; The Limits of Scripture: Vivekananda's Reinterpretation of the Authority of the Vedas; The Advaita Worldview: God, World and Humanity; A Hindu Theology of Liberation: Not-Two is Not-One; Essays in Hindu Theology;* and *Pathways to Hindu-Christian Dialogue.* He has also written commentaries on the Ramayana and the Bhagavadgita.

Prof. Rambachan has been involved in interreligious relations and dialogue for over 40 years, as a Hindu contributor and analyst. He is a Co-President of Religions for Peace.